Contents

KU-131-863

Weblink: www.science-at-school.com

What is a gas?

Gases are made of small PARTICLES that spread out to fill any space.

Ever wondered why a balloon makes a loud bang when it is popped? The answer is that the air rushes out of the hole at the speed of sound (Picture 1).

Air is a **GAS**. A gas is a **SUBSTANCE** that is spread so thinly you usually can't tell it's there. But the bursting balloon should convince you that gas is real enough!

Gas is very different from a **SOLID** or a **LIQUID**. Think about water, and you will see how different gas really is.

The water in an ice cube is solid – it holds its shape. Water can also be a liquid – it holds together, but takes the shape of whatever container it is in.

There is water in the air around you too. Here it is a gas. In this form, the water particles are spread out so thinly that you can't see or touch the water any longer. For example, when you boil water on the stove, it turns into a gas (steam) and enters the air.

Gases are made of the same substances as solids and liquids, but they are able to spread out to fill any space.

▼ **(Picture 1) The popping sound of a bursting balloon is caused by the air in the balloon rushing out very quickly.**

In a solid, all of the particles are locked together. They can't move, so the solid can't change shape without being pulled or pushed.

Science@School | Book 5C

Gases around us

A brief history

TODAY... 1898 The Pepsi-Cola Company is founded by Caleb D Bradham... 1886 Cola, a drink containing compressed carbon dioxide gas, is invented in Atlanta, USA, by John S Pemberton. It is later used as the first product of the Coca-Cola company... 1794 Jacob Schweppe, in Switzerland, begins to sell carbonated mineral water... 1777 French chemist Antoine Lavoisier coins the word oxygen, and discovers that it is a separate substance in the air... 1772 Daniel Rutherford, a British scientist, discovers nitrogen, the most common gas in the air... 1772 Oxygen is identified as a gas in air by Swedish chemist Karl Scheele... 1772 Joseph Priestley, a British scientist, was the first to obtain carbon dioxide. He developed apparatus for producing the gas from chemicals and adding it to water – the origin of the 'fizzy drink'... 1685 Robert Boyle, an Irish scientist and one of the founders of modern chemistry, describes artificial ways of imitating natural spring waters... 1670 Robert Boyle discovers a gas that burns – hydrogen. At first it is called inflammable air... 1662 Robert Boyle describes a law giving the relationship between the space gases take up (their volume) and the amount they are squeezed (the pressure on them)... 1620 The term gas is used by Belgian scientist Jan Baptist van Helmont to refer to all substances like air.

For more information visit www.science-at-school.com

Dr Brian Knapp

Word list

These are some science words that you should look out for as you go through the book. They are shown using CAPITAL letters.

ACID RAIN
Rain that has been polluted with acid gases made by burning fuels.

AIR POLLUTION
Air that has enough human-made gases and particles in it to create a haze, to make it smell, to make the throat and eyes smart, or to produce acid rain.

COMPRESSED AIR
Air that has been squashed so that the particles are closer together than they would naturally be.

CONCENTRATED
A place where there is a larger number of gas particles than elsewhere.

EVAPORATION
To turn from a liquid into a gas.

FUEL
A material that we burn in order to make electricity, to heat homes or to power transportation.

GAS
A form of a substance in which the particles are separate and free to move about. A gas spreads out to fill as much space as it can.

GLOBAL WARMING
The rapid rise in the world's temperatures due to human activities.

HEAT
A form of energy that causes the temperature to rise.

HUMID/HUMIDITY
Humid air contains enough moisture for it to be noticeable and make the air feel clammy.
   Humidity is the amount of moisture in the air compared with the maximum amount that the air could hold.

LIQUID
A form of a substance in which the particles are free to move about but are still loosely touching one another.

MIXTURE
A substance that is made of two or more substances that are not combined.

MOISTURE
Another word for water vapour.

PARTICLES
Pieces of a substance that are too small to be seen except with special microscopes. They are much smaller than dust.

SCENT
A gas that has a smell.

SOLID
A form of a substance where the particles are fixed together. As a result, a solid keeps a fixed shape unless it is pushed or pulled.

SUBSTANCE
A pure chemical from which other things can be made.

THERMAL
A rising flow of warm air caused by the heating of the ground.

VAPOUR
Another word for a gas.

WATER VAPOUR
The name given to water when it is in the form of a gas.

2

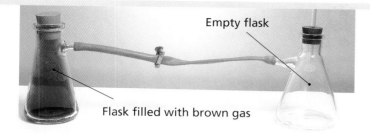
Empty flask

Flask filled with brown gas

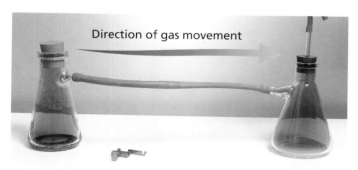
Direction of gas movement

▲ (Picture 2) Gases will rush to fill any space left empty. (Top) The flasks are kept separated by the clamp on the tube. (Bottom) As soon as the clamp was removed, the gas rushed from one flask to the other in less than a thousandth of a second.

How gases move

It's hard to see what air does because it is colourless. But scientists can show how gases move with a demonstration using a coloured gas (Picture 2).

In a gas, the particles are no longer attached to one another, but are moving freely around. They bounce into one another, pushing each other apart, until they are all evenly spaced. The more space there is for them to fill, the farther apart the particles will spread. A gas has no fixed size or shape and it can always take up more space than a solid or a liquid – usually a great deal more space.

In a liquid, all of the particles can slide past one another, so they have no fixed shape. Nevertheless, they take up about the same amount of space as the solid.

At the start of the demonstration, there are two glass flasks connected by a tube. The tube is clamped so that nothing can get from one flask to the other. In one glass flask the scientist puts a dark brown gas. All of the air in the other flask is pumped out, so it is completely empty.

What you see next seems to happen almost by magic. When the scientist takes the clamp off, in an instant both flasks are full of brown gas. The gas particles moved at 500 metres per second!

Both flasks are now completely full and exactly the same colour. But the gas in each flask is now a paler shade of brown, so the gas must be more thinly spread than when it was all trapped in just one flask. This tells us that the brown gas is now shared equally between the flasks and is less **CONCENTRATED**.

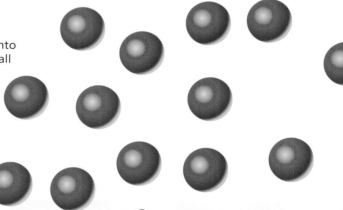

Summary

- Gases are made of particles that continually bounce off one another.
- Gases fill any space they can.
- When gases fill more space they become more spread out.

Weblink: www.science-at-school.com

How gases mix

Gases begin to mix the instant they come into contact.

The mixing of gases is very important. For example, if the gases you breathed out didn't mix with fresh air, you would keep breathing the same stale gas back in (Picture 1). In fact, the gases you breathe out immediately begin to mix with the gases in the air.

How mixing works

In Picture 2 you see what the mixing of gases is all about. In this case, a scientist put some brown gas in the bottom of a flask filled with air. The scientist then put a lid on the flask.

As you can see, the brown gas soon began to move up the

▼ **(Picture 1) When you breathe out, you push stale air a short distance away and breathe in air from close to your face. This gives the breathed-out gas time to mix with the air before you breathe it in again.**

▶ **(Picture 2) The stages of a brown gas mixing with air. Notice how the brown gas becomes a paler colour as it mixes.**

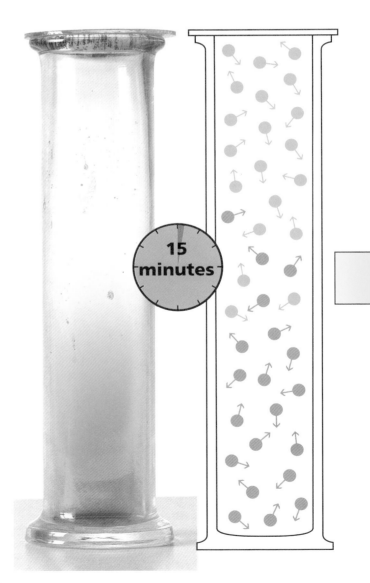

15 minutes

Weblink: www.science-at-school.com

jar, while the colourless air moved down. After five hours, the gases were completely mixed.

What happened?

Each gas spread throughout the whole jar. The brown gas moved towards the top of the flask and the air moved to the bottom. Of course, the particles of the two gases keep bumping in to each other, and so it took time for them to spread out.

This is an important fact about gases that we rely on all of the time. We expect the air, for example, to be the same wherever we go. The fact that it is like this is only possible because the gases in the air are continually bouncing about and mixing.

Summary

- Gases expand to fill as much space as they can.
- Gases mix evenly, even if one is heavier than the other.
- When gases mix, each gas becomes more spread out.

Weblink: www.science-at-school.com

How scents travel

Gases move easily. SCENTS are gas particles we can smell that are carried along by the air.

Anything that we can smell is a gas. The gas may start off as a liquid perfume that you put on your skin, as solid blocks of air freshener placed in a room, or on the petals of a flower, but to become a scent the substance has to change steadily into a gas.

Scents move about easily and quickly

On pages 6 and 7 we saw how good the air is at mixing with gases. This is why you can often smell what is being cooked in the kitchen before you see the food.

The reason that a scent, or an unpleasant smell, can travel is that the air is not completely filled with gases. There is still plenty of room for new particles of gas to get into the air and then move around.

Left undisturbed, gases will mix themselves up evenly. However, when a new gas enters the air (Picture 1) it is concentrated just at one place. It immediately begins to spread out so that it, too, becomes evenly mixed in the air (Picture 2). This means that the scent of a flower spreads out all around the flower – in the same way that food smells will spread all around a kitchen.

▼ (Picture 2) In still air, particles of a scent gradually spread out in all directions. The more they spread out, the less concentrated they become, and so they are harder to smell.

◄ (Picture 1) The scent from a flower starts by being concentrated in the flower.

8

Why scents fade away

Have you noticed how a perfume sprayed onto your hand smells strongly for a while and then fades away? Or how the smell of cooking gradually disappears? This happens because the gases of the scent from the perfume and the cooking gradually mix with air and become less concentrated.

Our noses are only good at smelling quite concentrated gases, so after a while, although the gases produced by the flower and during cooking are still there, they have become spread so thinly that we don't notice them.

A dog, which has a much more sensitive nose, will still be able to smell gases when they have become far too faint for us (Picture 3).

The effect of a breeze

When a breeze blows, the air is no longer still, but is flowing in one direction. This means that the scent particles are carried along in the same direction as the air (Picture 4). As a result, they form a long stream of particles, and the scent can only be smelled from one direction. Insects follow

this stream of scent back to the flower. Other animals follow scents to the source of their favourite foods.

▲ **(Picture 4) When a breeze blows, the scent will still spread out. The moving air will carry the scent in only one direction, but it can be smelled from further away.**

Summary

- A scent is a gas we can smell.
- Scents mix with the air, so we can breathe them in.
- Scents spread out over time, until they are too faint for us to smell.

▶ **(Picture 3) Dogs have noses that are much more sensitive to the smells of gases than humans.**

Weblink: www.science-at-school.com

Hot air swells and rises

When air is heated it gets lighter and rises. This is why the gases from a fire go up a chimney, why hot air balloons work and even why the clouds float.

Have you ever watched the sparks and flames flickering up from a bonfire? They don't go sideways or down, they go up.

The sparks and smoke are being carried up by invisible hot air.

Whenever air gets hot it swells and becomes lighter. Because warm air is lighter, it rises.

Rising air detector

Because the air is invisible, it is difficult to see it rising. But a light bulb will warm enough air to turn a paper windmill (Picture 1). The windmill turns because the air is rising and flowing past the blades.

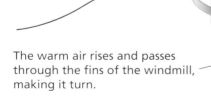

The warm air rises and passes through the fins of the windmill, making it turn.

A light bulb provides a source of heat, warming the air above it.

Hot air balloon

A hot air balloon is another way of seeing hot air on the move. In this case, the balloonist blows hot air into the balloon. The hot air gets trapped inside the balloon and it rises, lifting the balloon and basket off the ground (Picture 2).

Clouds

Air does not have to be very hot before it starts to rise. It only has to be slightly warmer than its surroundings.

Nature can produce some spectacular displays when slightly warmed air rises. Pilots in aeroplanes call such rising air **THERMALS**, and when this rising air carries droplets of water, it forms clouds (Picture 3).

In this case, the shape of the cloud shows us the shape of the rising hot air, which is not unlike a hot air balloon, is it?

◀ **(Picture 1) This small windmill detects rising air. It will work over a light bulb or a room radiator.**

Weblink: www.science-at-school.com

▼ (Picture 2) The stages in lifting a hot air balloon.

The balloonist uses a gas flame to heat air and fill the balloon.

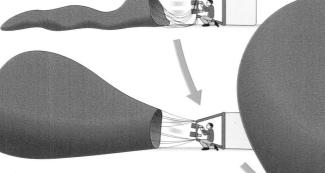

The balloonist can change the height of the balloon by adding more heat.

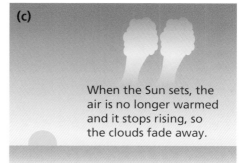

(a)

Rising air forms invisible thermals.

(b) Visible clouds

Invisible **WATER VAPOUR** mixed in the air turns to droplets and makes clouds visible above this height.

(c)

When the Sun sets, the air is no longer warmed and it stops rising, so the clouds fade away.

▲ (Picture 3) How bubbling clouds are formed on still, sunny days.
(a) Air is warmed by the Sun each day.
(b) The warmed air begins to rise and clouds form.
(c) When the Sun sets and no longer warms the land, the air stops rising and no new clouds are formed.

Summary

• Warm air rises.
• Warm air takes up more space than cool air.
• Clouds are formed when warm air rises.

Weblink: www.science-at-school.com

Moisture and evaporation

MOISTURE gets into the air by EVAPORATION.

The air contains invisible water. We call this moisture **WATER VAPOUR**.

You cannot see, smell or taste water vapour – but it's there. However, you can sometimes sense that there is a lot of water in the air. We then say that it feels **HUMID**. The air above a heated indoor swimming pool, for example, feels humid because it contains lots of water vapour.

Measuring humidity

There are instruments to tell you the amount of moisture in the air. One of these is called a hygrometer (Picture 1). It uses a piece of hair, because hair gets longer in damp air.

▼ **(Picture 1) A hygrometer uses a long human hair to measure the moisture in the air! You can make one of these. Just make sure the pin used as a pivot is much closer to the end with the hair attached. The hygrometer will only work in an upright position, such as fixed to a wall.**

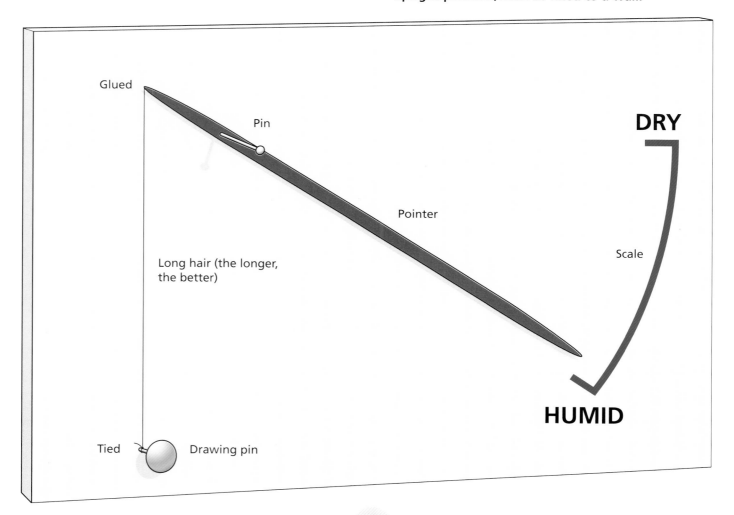

(Picture 2) As the water in this kettle boils, it evaporates and turns to water vapour (steam) and enters the air.

Evaporation – disappearing water

Water gets into the air by changing from a liquid to a gas. This change is called evaporation (Picture 2).

(Picture 3) As a puddle dries, water particles leave the water and go into the air. Once they are in the air they begin to mix with all of the other gases.

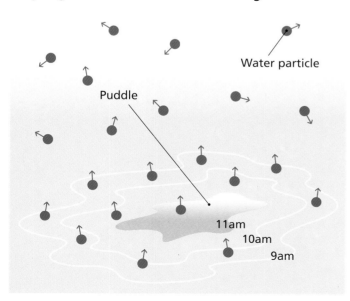

Water particle

Puddle

11am
10am
9am

(Picture 4) If you fill a glass measuring cylinder with water and mark the level each day, you can measure the amount of evaporation. The evaporation should get slower as the water level goes down. Can you think why this should be?

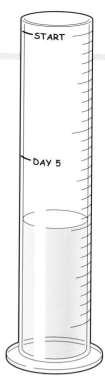

START

DAY 5

You cannot see the water evaporating because each particle is too small. But you can see the results, for example, by marking the edges of a puddle with chalk as it dries (Picture 3), or by marking the changes in water level in a tall water-filled jar (Picture 4).

What affects evaporation?

Here are the things that affect the speed at which water can become a gas:

1. Warm air can hold more moisture than cold air.
2. Dry air will take up moisture more quickly than moist air.
3. Moving air, such as a breeze, will take up moisture more quickly than still air.

Summary

- Water vapour is moisture in the air.
- Liquid water changes to water vapour in a process called evaporation.
- Water evaporates faster when the air is dry, warm and when there is a good breeze.

Weblink: www.science-at-school.com

Gas bubbles

Bubbles are gas trapped inside liquid skins.

Most of the gases around us are free to move about. But sometimes the gases become trapped, and this is when they form bubbles.

Remember that in a liquid all of the particles are touching. It is as though they were all chained together. This is why, when you put a drop of water on a surface, it doesn't spread out, but stays together as a droplet (Picture 1).

Now imagine what happens when air gets inside water. The water still tries to stay together, and so it traps the gas in a ball – this is what we call a bubble (Picture 2).

Bubbles in water

A gas is much lighter than a liquid. Any gas trapped in a liquid will therefore rise to the surface. For example, when you squeeze a sponge under water and force out any trapped air, the air rises as bubbles.

Fizzy drink bubbles

Another place you will see bubbles is when you open a bottle of fizzy drink. Streams of bubbles rise up through the drink and burst on the surface (Picture 3). In this case the gas is not air, but carbon dioxide that was forced into the liquid during manufacture.

▶ (Picture 1) A water droplet in air forms a small ball.

◀▼ (Picture 2) Gas trapped inside water also forms as balls – called bubbles.

▶ (Picture 3) Gas bubbles rising to the surface in a fizzy drink. As the bubbles rise, they get bigger. This happens because the pressure of the liquid is less near the surface than lower down in the bottle.

Soap bubbles

Soap bubbles are remarkable because they do not burst on the surface like bubbles in water. The soap film is strong enough to prevent the air from getting out.

Small soap bubbles will last for a long time – we call this lather. But if you blow bubbles, you make the bubble much more fragile. As the bubble gets bigger, the soap film gets thinner and thinner until finally there is not enough soap to go around and the bubble bursts (Picture 4).

Soap bubbles gently fall through the air because the soap film makes the bubble heavier than air.

Make your own bubbles

You can easily make your own bubbles by taking a piece of chalk (not blackboard chalk) or lime from a garden centre and pouring vinegar over it. The gas formed is carbon dioxide.

Vinegar

Lump of chalk

Carbon dioxide gas bubbles

Summary

- Gases form bubbles when trapped inside liquids.
- Bubbles grow as they rise through a liquid.
- Soap bubbles are gases surrounded by a soap film.

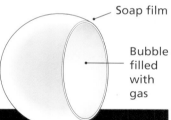

▼▶ (Picture 4) Blowing soap bubbles stretches the soap film because the gas (air) inside the film is compressed and tries to expand.

Soap film

Bubble filled with gas

Weblink: www.science-at-school.com

What is in the air?

Air is a mixture of invisible, tasteless and colourless gases.

You cannot see, smell or touch air, but you know from the previous pages that air is always on the move.

Usually we think of the air as being just one thing. But the air around you is really a **MIXTURE** of gases (Picture 1).

The most common gas in the air is called nitrogen (Picture 2). Nitrogen is not necessary for breathing, and does not affect most materials, so you can think of it as a kind of filler.

About one-fifth of the air is oxygen. Oxygen is quite different to nitrogen – it changes almost everything it touches. Oxygen makes damp iron go rusty, it is necessary for fires to start and all animals need it to live (see pages 18 to 19).

Other gases occur in small amounts in the air. Nevertheless, some are very important. Water is found in the air as

▶ **(Picture 1) The air is made of a mixture of gases. Most gases are made of tiny, colourless PARTICLES. Particles of pollution, on the other hand, are sometimes coloured, and we can see these parts of the air as a brown haze.**

A tiny amount of the air is helium and other rare gases.

A small amount of the air is water vapour (normally less than 1 part in a 100). See page 12.

A very small amount of the air is carbon dioxide (less than 1 part in 300). See page 18.

Most of the air is made of nitrogen (78 out of every 100 parts of the air).

A fifth of the air is made of oxygen (21 out of every 100 parts of the air). See page 18.

A small (variable) part of the air may be particles of pollution. See page 20.

Note: The air in a typical room of your house contains 10,000,000,000,000,000,000,000,000,000 gas particles!

a gas, or **VAPOUR**. This gets carried high into the sky and makes clouds. This gas is important to rain.

Carbon dioxide is another important gas that occurs in the air in small amounts. It is vital to plant growth, and it also keeps the air warm by soaking up heat from the Sun (see pages 18 to 19). The other gases in the air occur in really tiny amounts. Some of them, like helium and neon (Picture 3), are used for special purposes.

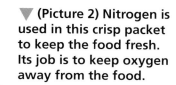

▼ (Picture 2) Nitrogen is used in this crisp packet to keep the food fresh. Its job is to keep oxygen away from the food.

▶ (Picture 3) Helium is lighter than air and is sometimes used in balloons to make them float.

Weighing gas

In an ordinary living room there are a vast number of gas particles. Each one is incredibly tiny, but if you could weigh them all, you would find they came to a staggering 80kg! But you can more easily measure the weight of air by squashing some of it into a small space. One way of doing this is to blow up a balloon. The balloon is now filled with squashed air, called **COMPRESSED AIR**. If you compare the weight of the air-filled balloon with the weight of a balloon with no air in it, you will find that the balloon containing the compressed air is heavier – it makes one side of a balance tip down (Picture 4).

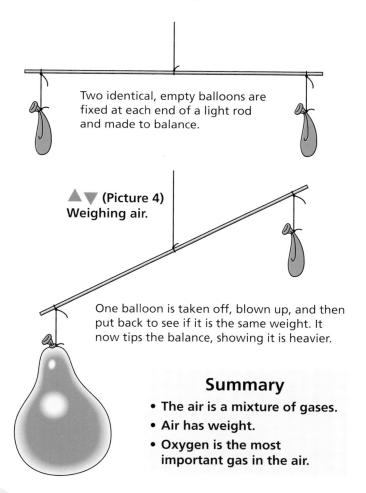

Two identical, empty balloons are fixed at each end of a light rod and made to balance.

▲▼ (Picture 4) Weighing air.

One balloon is taken off, blown up, and then put back to see if it is the same weight. It now tips the balance, showing it is heavier.

Summary
- The air is a mixture of gases.
- Air has weight.
- Oxygen is the most important gas in the air.

Weblink: www.science-at-school.com

Oxygen and carbon dioxide

Two of the gases in the air are vital to all living things.

The air contains two gases that affect our day to day lives. They are oxygen and carbon dioxide.

Oxygen

Oxygen makes up one-fifth of all the gas in the air. Oxygen combines with many things. When it does this quickly, the effect can be dramatic. This is what happens in a fire (Picture 1). When oxygen combines more slowly with metals it causes them to lose their shine. In our bodies, oxygen combines with food to release the energy that sustains us (Picture 2).

When oxygen combines with food in our blood, a new gas is made, called carbon dioxide. We breathe in oxygen and breathe out carbon dioxide.

Carbon dioxide

Every leaf, stem and flower that you see has been made using carbon dioxide. Plants need carbon dioxide just like we need oxygen. As carbon dioxide is used by plants they release oxygen (Picture 2 on page 14).

The oxygen cycle

There is a never-ending cycle that keeps the amounts of carbon dioxide and

▲ (Picture 1) Oxygen easily combines with many other substances, giving out heat. This is how our bodies stay warm, but if it happens very quickly, and if it starts at a very high temperature, then things catch fire!

▼ (Picture 2) Oxygen is vital to life on Earth. We need oxygen to breathe. There is no oxygen in space, so astronauts need to provide their own supply.

Weblink: www.science-at-school.com

oxygen in the world balanced. Plants use carbon dioxide and produce oxygen as they grow. Animals use the oxygen to grow and give out carbon dioxide which the plants use (Picture 3). This is called the oxygen cycle.

Global warming

Unlike most other gases, carbon dioxide soaks up **HEAT**. The more carbon dioxide there is in the air, the warmer the air becomes.

Over millions of years, great forests have become buried and turned into coal, while animal remains have been buried and turned into oil and natural gas. These burials locked up lots of carbon and so removed carbon dioxide from the cycle.

Burning coal, oil and natural gas releases carbon dioxide back into the air, allowing the air to soak up more heat. This warming of our air in recent times has been called **GLOBAL WARMING**. Scientists are now worried that this rapid change may alter the climate across the world.

Summary

- Oxygen combines with many substances, often releasing heat.
- Carbon dioxide is needed by plants.
- Oxygen and carbon dioxide are renewed in a continuous cycle.

▼ (Picture 3) The oxygen cycle.

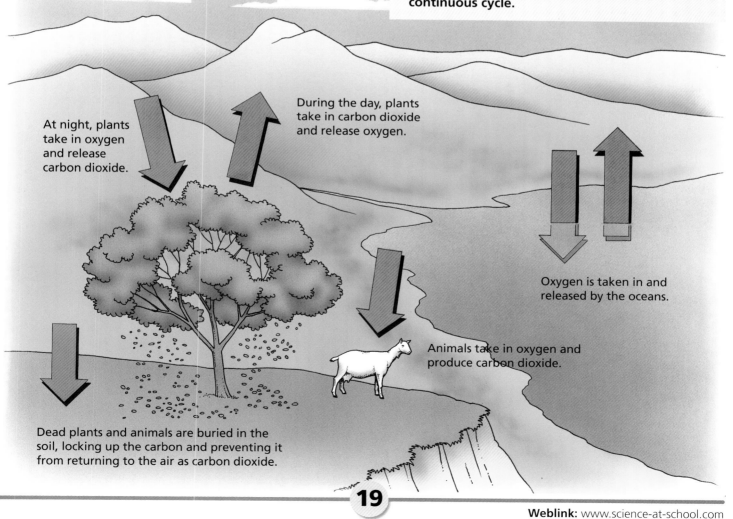

At night, plants take in oxygen and release carbon dioxide.

During the day, plants take in carbon dioxide and release oxygen.

Oxygen is taken in and released by the oceans.

Animals take in oxygen and produce carbon dioxide.

Dead plants and animals are buried in the soil, locking up the carbon and preventing it from returning to the air as carbon dioxide.

Weblink: www.science-at-school.com

Air pollution

Air pollution is caused by unwanted, and often harmful, gases in the air.

On pages 8 and 9 we saw how easy it is for a scent to travel. Unpleasant, and even harmful, gases can travel just as quickly. These gases produce **AIR POLLUTION**.

Polluting gases around us

Air pollution is caused by air becoming mixed with gases that are unpleasant, irritating or that can do us harm.

The main gases that pollute our air are released (along with carbon dioxide) when we burn coal, oil and natural gas. The major gases produced this way are called sulphur dioxide, nitrogen dioxide and ozone.

Power station gases

Coal, oil and gas all contain a substance called sulphur. When one of these fuels burns, the sulphur combines with the oxygen in the air to make a gas called sulphur dioxide.

Water droplets in clouds soak up the sulphur dioxide gas. When this happens, the water becomes acid. When it then falls as rain we call it **ACID RAIN**. When acid rain falls onto plants, or gets into the soil, plants are harmed and can even die. There are many forests in Europe and North America that have been killed by acid rain.

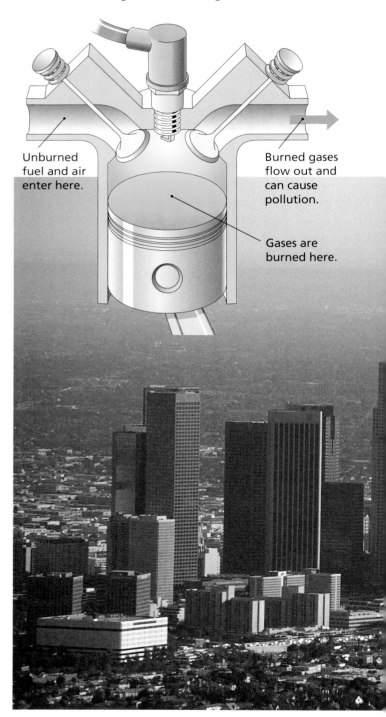

▼ (Picture 1) When fuel burns inside an engine, oxygen and nitrogen combine to form a reddish-brown gas called nitrogen dioxide.

Unburned fuel and air enter here.

Burned gases flow out and can cause pollution.

Gases are burned here.

Weblink: www.science-at-school.com

Vehicle fumes

Engines work by sucking in a mixture of air and fuel, and then burning it (Picture 1). This produces a brown gas called nitrogen dioxide. This brown gas helps to cause the brown haze that hangs over cities on hot, still summer days (Picture 2).

At the same time, the fumes cause some oxygen in the air to change to a new gas called ozone (Picture 3). Ozone is a vital gas high in the sky (where it protects us from dangerous rays in sunshine) but at street level it makes eyes hurt and throats sting. Cars fitted with a special type of exhaust, called a catalytic converter, prevent much of this pollution. This is why all new cars have these converters fitted.

Summary

- Air pollution is caused by unpleasant and harmful gases in the air.
- Sulphur gases cause acid rain.
- Nitrogen dioxide gas produces a brown haze in the air.

(Picture 2) You can see the haze produced by nitrogen dioxide in the picture below.

(Picture 3) This bus seems to be sending out just soot, but it is also rich in invisible ozone and nitrogen gases.

Weblink: www.science-at-school.com

Energy from gases

When FUELS are heated they give off a gas. The gas mixes with oxygen in the air and catches fire. This is burning.

A gas that can be used for energy is called a fuel. Most people cook or heat their homes using gases. If you have gas cooking, gas or oil central heating, or a coal, wood or oil-fired kitchen oven then you actually cook with gas!

In the past, people have also lit their homes using gas, because a candle works by giving off a gas that burns in air.

Candle power

A candle contains a flammable wick (Picture 1). When the wick is lit, the heat from the wick turns the candle wax into a gas. The hot gas mixes with the oxygen in the air and begins to burn, giving out light and heat.

It is easy to show that both oxygen and a gas are needed for burning. If a glass jar is placed over a burning candle, so that no new oxygen can reach the candle, the candle will quickly go out (Picture 2). This shows it is not the wick that keeps the candle burning, but the oxygen in the air.

Heat or light?

Have you noticed how a gas stove burns with a blue flame and a candle burns with a yellow flame? This is not an accident. The candle is used to give out light, whereas the stove is designed to give out heat.

▲ (Picture 1) A candle burns by turning the wax into a vapour which mixes with the air.

▲ (Picture 2) Without air a candle goes out, showing that something in air is vital for burning.

Weblink: www.science-at-school.com

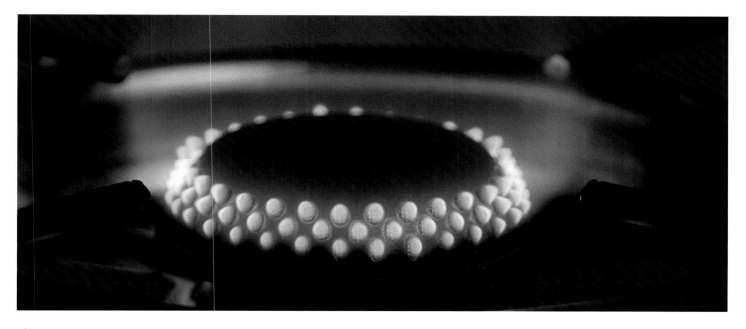

▲ (Picture 3) This is a gas stove in operation. The gas and air mix is designed to give out as much heat as possible.

▼ (Picture 4) A rocket taking the Space Shuttle into space. Compressed oxygen is carried with the fuel because there is no air in space.

A candle burns brightly because the wax vapour doesn't mix very well with the oxygen in the air around it.

A gas stove (Picture 3) burns with a pale blue light (and gives out much more heat) because the many holes in the burners are designed to mix the stove gases and the air much better.

Rocket fuel

Many gases can be used as fuels. One of the most powerful is hydrogen gas. Hydrogen and oxygen are mixed together in rocket engines to give rockets enough power to lift into space (Picture 4).

Summary

- Gases can be used as fuels.
- Oxygen, as well as the fuel gas, is needed before the gas will give out heat or light.

Weblink: www.science-at-school.com

Index

Science@School

Science@School is a series published by Atlantic Europe Publishing Company Ltd.

Atlantic Europe Publishing

Teacher's Guide
There is a Teacher's Guide with activity and comprehension worksheets to accompany this book.

CD-ROMs
There are some browser-based CD-ROMs containing information to support the Science@School series.

Dedicated Web Site
There's more information about other great Science@School packs and a wealth of supporting material available at our dedicated web site:

www.science-at-school.com

First published in 2002 by
Atlantic Europe Publishing Company Ltd

Copyright © 2002
Atlantic Europe Publishing Company Ltd
First reprint 2006

All rights reserved. No part of this publication may be reproduced, stored in a retrieval system, or transmitted in any form or by any means, electronic, mechanical, photocopying, recording or otherwise, without prior permission of the publisher.

Author
Brian Knapp, BSc, PhD

Educational Consultant
Peter Riley, BSc, C Biol, MI Biol, PGCE

Art Director
Duncan McCrae, BSc

Senior Designer
Adele Humphries, BA, PGCE

Editor
Lisa Magloff, BA

Illustrations
David Woodroffe

Designed and produced by
EARTHSCAPE EDITIONS

Reproduced by
Global Colour

Printed in China by
WKT Co., Ltd

Science@School
Volume 5C *Gases around us*
A CIP record for this book is available from the British Library.
ISBN-10: 1-86214-156-8
ISBN-13: 978-1-86214-156-8

Picture credits
All photographs are from the Earthscape Editions photolibrary, except the following: (c=centre t=top b=bottom l=left r=right) Fire Research Station Borehamwood 18t; NASA 18br, 23br.

This product is manufactured from sustainable managed forests. For every tree cut down at least one more is planted.